THE
Archive Photographs
SERIES

SOUTH WALES
FROM THE BUSH COLLECTION
VOLUME II

Mr Ernest Thomas Bush (1876-1930).

THE
Archive Photographs
SERIES

SOUTH WALES
FROM THE BUSH COLLECTION
VOLUME II

Compiled by
Derek Warry

CHALFORD

The Chalford Publishing Company
St Mary's Mill, Chalford,
Stroud, Gloucestershire, GL6 8NX

ISBN 0 7524 1126 8

Typesetting and origination by
The Chalford Publishing Company
Printed in Great Britain by
Bailey Print, Dursley, Gloucestershire

*Dedicated to my wife Lynne in appreciation
for her understanding of my obsession*

Contents

Thomastown post office, in The Square, Thomastown, *c.* 1911.

Introduction

It is my pleasure to introduce a second volume of photographs from the Bush Collection.

I first met Derek Warry over fifteen years ago when his enthusiasm for the photographs taken by photographer Ernest Bush led him to research Bush's early roots in Cardiff. Derek arrived on the doorstep of my mother's house armed with a bunch of flowers and a string of endless questions about the elusive Mr Bush. The collector's enthusiasm for his subject and his delight at discovering recollections of the Bush family were infectious. Imagine our surprise on being shown just a selection of the vast number of Ernest Bush's postcards that had been produced in the early part of the century.

As a child, I was aware of a collection of brown sepia family photographs obviously taken by a professional photographer and frequently featuring a gentleman sporting his straw boater and a bow tie. Enquiry revealed that this natty dresser was my grandfather's only brother who had been a photographer in Cardiff. An intriguing entry in the family Bible disclosed that Ernest Bush had died on 25th November 1930. There was somehow a hint of the dissolute, in dying in a Blackpool hotel at the relatively young age of 54, when all the rest of the family had died respectably in their beds in Cardiff. All attempts to unearth more details were greeted with tight-lipped silence. This response suggested that Ernest Bush had been regarded as the black sheep of the family.

Not for him the respectability of an office job! The rest of the family were all closely linked with Cardiff docks which at that time were experiencing the height of the coal exporting boom. Ernest Bush's father, George Bush, had been head of the vast array of coaling cranes which feature in so many of the photographs of the docks at that time. His brother, David George Bush, spent forty-seven years at the docks, beginning as a clerk to the Trustees of the Marquis of Bute, and retiring as chief of the commercial department of The Great Western Railway at the docks. Later his son, Oscar Bush, who was my father, worked there. Perhaps it was thought that Ernest Bush should have followed a similar path rather than pursue the relatively new and somewhat risqué career as a photographer.

The hub of Cardiff's commercial life was centred on its docks, the ships and the ship owners during the early years of this century, but this prosperity soon came to an end. Today it is the photographs taken by Ernest Bush that provide a lasting portrayal, not only of the centre of Cardiff and its burgeoning suburbs, but also of the towns and villages throughout South Wales. These photographs depict the industrial and rural past of so many communities, with that ubiquitous straw boater popping up in the most unlikely places!

It is thanks to the dedicated collecting and painstaking cataloguing of Derek Warry that the Bush collection has been assembled and made available to the public in this series of Archive Photographs.

Pamela Haines (née Bush)

One
West Wales

Charles Street, Milford Haven. The establishments of Charles Herbert Whicher outfitter, and Cash & Co. boot and shoe makers, are clearly visible in this picture of Charles Street, c. 1908. (2241)

General View (No. 2) Haverfordwest. This card taken in Haverfordwest, in Welsh Hwlford, shows the stone bridge with three arches over the river Cleddau, *c.* 1914. The town had some good shops but was chiefly dependent upon the agricultural neighbourhood for support. A considerable trade was done in corn, butter, seeds and manure as well as malting, brewing, currying and timber. (3886)

The Priory ruins from the Parade, Haverfordwest. The Priory is that of St Mary and St Thomas the Martyr, and was founded by Robert de Hwlford, second holder of the Lordship of Haverfordwest, before 1200 AD. The wooden bridge on the left is on the main Great Western Railway line and was constructed so that the centre lifted to allow vessels to pass without demasting. (3885)

The Bridge, Carmarthen, c. 1914. The stone bridge with seven arches over the river Towy. The river was celebrated for its salmon and trout and also for its boats made of wicker work, which were covered with pitched canvas, and known as coracles. On the left the Co-operative Society Ltd building can be seen. (3899)

The Guildhall, Carmarthen, c. 1914. The Shire Hall, as it was known, was built in 1582 and renovated in 1909 at a cost of £2,000. The monument in the centre was erected in 1905 to the memory of the volunteers of the town who fell in the South African War. Archibald Hodges boot and shoemaker, is on the left of the square. (3895)

The Forge, Kidwelly. Two children on the wall enjoy having their photograph taken outside The Forge, c. 1920. Our photographer had traveled a long way from Cardiff for this series of photographs. (4179)

Bridge Street, Kidwelly. The four lads look as if they are barring the way into town, c. 1920. (4180)

Lady Street, Kidwelly. The policeman on the right stands smartly to attention in this picture of Lady Street, *c.* 1920. Who is the gentleman in the straw boater? Could this be the same person who appears in several other cards? (4176)

High Street, Llandebie. This village on the road from Llandilo Fawr to Llanelly, in the old county of Carmarthen, had a population of 5,607 when this picture was taken, *c.* 1920. Note the chemist shop of David John Lewis. (4124)

The Village (No. 1), Penygroes. A peaceful village scene, *c.* 1909. Note the gentleman looking out of place in a three piece suit and straw boater outside the building on the left. Could he be part of the Bush entourage? (2606)

Villiers Street, Briton Ferry. Typically the whole street was watching Mr Bush take this picture of Villers Street, *c.* 1920. Note Charles Bazzard & Son colliery agents above the bank and opposite Jones and Co. clothiers of 39 Villiers Street. (4229)

Station Road, Burry Port. Jockeys Ales are clearly advertised at the Railway Hotel where Mrs Elizabeth Watkins was proprietor. Again note the gentleman outside the newsagents. Could he be the same one that is in card No. 2606, p. 14? (3270)

Station Road, Llanelly, *c.* 1924. A tram trundles past the ladies' and gentlemen's hairdressers and the crossroads in Station Road. This is one of the later cards published by the Bush photographic company. (5260)

Stephany Street, Llanelly, *c.* 1924. This shows The York Hotel on the left, managed by Alexander W. Wilson. On the right can be seen the Billiard Hall and Harper and Preece fruiterer's, of 84 Stephany Street. (5256)

Parkmill (No. 2), Swansea. An interesting picture of Parkmill, *c.* 1910. Note the policeman on the left who seems to be making a note in his book. Surely not issuing a parking ticket for the horse and cart? Also note Mr 'Straw Boater' again. (3354)

Sketty Village (No. 1), Swansea, *c.* 1911. It is no surprise that he took this picture of Gower Road with the Bush Inn showing on the left of the picture where Horace Cutcliffe was manager. (3188)

The Beach, Langland Bay. Beach huts and bowler hats, but not much sun, can be seen on the beach at Langland Bay, *c.* 1911. (2954)

General View, Mumbles. John Eley, family butcher at the Dunns, Mumbles is clearly advertised in this general view, *c*. 1910. Mr Bush was very fond of his 'General Views'. (2636)

The Pier, Mumbles. A paddle steamer is at the end of the pier as the Mumbles train leaves, *c*. 1911. Note the number of ships in the channel. (3115)

Castle Street, Swansea. Cream ices at 3d and 6d are advertised at R. E. Jones, Castle Café at 13 Castle Street, *c.* 1914. Next to the café, at No. 12, is the sale notice of Thomas Palmer Taylor. (3990)

Oxford Street, Swansea. A tram heading for Brynmill passes down Oxford Street, *c.* 1911. Note the Empire music hall adjacent to the Empire vaults and The Mansel Arms. Also prominent in this picture are Templer Malins advertising artificial teeth at No. 240, Martin Thomas' Piano Forte dealership at No. 241, ices from Miss Annie T Henwood at No. 239, Jones and Morgan house furnisher's at No. 238 and John Samuel Brown Motor Engineer at No. 237. (3327)

High Street (No. 3), Swansea. The Peoples Bioscope Palace, formally called the Palace Theatre of Varieties, is clearly visible in the centre of this picture of High Street, c. 1911. It was erected in 1901 at a cost of £30,000 and had seating for 2,500. (3329)

The Hospital, Swansea. A horse drawn carriage can be seen approaching the front of the hospital in St Helens Road as a tram heads for the High Street passing the hospital gates, c. 1912. (3881)

Pentyla, Port Talbot. A group of small boys appear amused as Mr Bush takes this picture in Pentyla, *c.* 1912. Around the corner shop on the left is the characteristic street advertising of the time. (3793)

Station Road (No. 3), Port Talbot. Llewellyn Bros house furnisher's, Davies & Hill draper's and W. Lewis photographer, all ply their trade in Station Street, *c.* 1912. (3786)

Port Talbot. One of a large number of multiviews published by Ernest Bush. This one includes the photographs No. 3781, 3794, 3780, which are also included in this volume. (3809)

MARGAM CASTLE.

SANDS AND PIER.

23

Station Road (No. 1), Port Talbot. Mr John H. Davies was the proprietor of The Grand Hotel when this picture was taken in about 1912. (3781)

Margam Castle, Port Talbot, *c.* 1915. This castle was built in the tudor style in 1830, and the surrounding park was seven miles in circumference. Miss Talbot was the lady of the manor and sole landowner. (3794)

Two

Valley and Vale

Coronation Road, Aberkenfig. The title should read 'Coronation Street', Aberkenfig. Not to be confused with a more famous 'Coronation Street', this cul de sac has no Rovers Return and no road surface. The X over the house on the right marks No. 32 where the writer of the card was staying when it was written on 24 August 1916. (3497)

Evanstown, Aberkenfig, *c.* 1916. For once the children, so nicely dressed in straw hats, seem oblivious to having their picture captured on film. (3500)

King Edward Street (No. 2), Blaengarw. Phillips Tea and Lyons Tea compete for the business in King Edward Street, *c.* 1913. Note the postcards decorating the shop window. (3848)

Blaengarw Road, Blaengarw. A horse and cart and a sack truck are the only two vehicles in this bleak scene in Blangarw, *c.* 1913. I wonder if the child is big enough to read the posters on the hoarding. (3853)

Aubrey Arms and Gough Avenue, Ystalyfera. Tree trunks and a canal bridge make up this peaceful scene, *c.* 1911. You can see the six spectators all 'watching the birdie'. (3736)

Station Road, Ystalyfera. The billboard outside Sam Baker, newsagent stationer and tobacconist where all kinds of London daily papers and magazines are supplied, proclaims: 'Wild Scenes at Llanelly Railway Meeting: Platform Stormed'. This headline probably refers to the storming of Llanelly station platform on the 18 August 1911. The railway men at a mass meeting on 19 August 1911 were ordered 'to down tools wherever you may be as soon as you receive the signal'. In the following confusion, strikers invaded the platform and jeered at the driver and stoker on the mail train from Neyland to Paddington telling them to 'come off the train'. Their appeals failed, however, and the train proceeded. This information, enables the dating of Mr Bush's postcards to be reassessed. (3732)

Vardre Road, Clydach. Vardre Road can be seen here as an unmade road with puddles and track marks showing that it was a well used thoroughfare, giving an interesting insight into life in Clydach, *c.* 1911. (3660)

The Square, Thomastown. Miss Fanny Johns was the proprietor of the Thomastown post office, and Mr John Harris owned The Ely Hotel, both pictured in this card, *c.* 1911. Note the long white apron on the lady hiding around the corner of the hotel. (3501)

Top Commercial Street, Maesteg. A lone cyclist rides past the New Theatre, Commercial Street, *c.* 1914, where the play *Not a Word* is being performed. The Army and Navy boot and clothing stores can be seen next to the Hotel. (3962)

Salisbury Road, Maesteg. Terraced houses overlook the railway line alongside Salisbury Road, *c.* 1907 (2341)

New Road, Porthcawl. Mr Walter E. Gardner, the grocer, is in the background and in the foreground the children are looking at the man in a straw boater and not at the camera! Is this man again part of the Bush photographic team? (3800)

The Esplanade, Porthcawl. A tranquil scene on the Esplanade. Note the young men with their walking sticks and the ladies with posh frocks entering the picture on the right. (3148)

Children bathing, Porthcawl. The water looks really cold with most of the children only going up to their ankles, the others on the bank prefer to watch. (3152)

Bridgend Road (No. 1), Pencoed, c. 1909. Mr Richard Thomas, proprieter of The Old King's Head, on the left, offers commercial accommodation, motor garage and pit, and stabling. (2716)

Bridgend Road (No. 3), Pencoed, *c.* 1909. (2718)
These two pictures show the rural nature of Pencoed in the early part of this century.

Tymerchant (No. 2), Pencoed, *c.* 1911. (3709)

Wimbourne Road, Pencoed. A fine vehicle, complete with klaxon horn in Wimbourne Road, *c*. 1911. Could this possibly be the transport used by Mr Bush? (3711)

4268   The South Village, Llanharry.   Ernest T.Bush

The South Village, Llanharry, *c*. 1920. (4268)

The church, Llantwit Major. Llantwit Major church is said to have been founded as a 'church and college' by St Illtyd, one of the earliest missionaries from Rome to Britain. This picture shows the church complete with its rural backyard.(2818)

The Pool, Barry Island. Everyone is posing and perambulating around the pool at Barry Island, c. 1909. The total lack of commercialisation is worthy of note. (2535)

Court Road, Cadoxton. John H. Venn was a saddler and cycle agent at No. 189 Court Road. Opposite is the Baptist church, *c.* 1911. (3753)

St Cadoc's church, Old Village, Cadoxton. The Revd John Smith-Longdon MA was rector of St Cadoc's church when this was taken in about 1912. The Three Bells Inn, free house, stands adjacent to it. (3750)

The Village (No. 2), Leckwith. This picture shows the rural nature of the village at Leckwith, *c.* 1909. The old water pump can be seen in the centre foreground. (3046)

The Old Thatched Cottage – Dinas Powis.

The Old Thatched Cottage, Dinas Powis. This is a card in The Bush Series taken around 1902. The cottage, known as Bay Tree Cottage, was the home of Mrs Ann Fowler who stitched shirts. It was occupied after the First World War, by Mrs E.M. Lewis. The house was unfortunately destroyed by fire in the 1920s. The thatch caught fire on Guy Fawkes night. Mrs Lewis fled, rescuing her most prized possessions – two bronze plaques commemorating the sacrifice of her sons, Frank and John, who were lost in the war. (1028)

Miss Gertrude Jenner (Copyright), Wenvoe. This is another postcard in the Bush Series and one of two cards of Gertrude Jenner, both of which bear a copyright reference. The original photographs are attributed to W. Booth so why they appear in this series is not known.

Gertrude Jenner was the oldest unmarried daughter of Mr Robert Francis Jenner, owner of Wenvoe Castle. She was born at Wenvoe Castle on 8 March 1835 and was brought up there, receiving a good education. She was considered an excellent Latin scholar.

Her father left his estate to her elder brother who subsequently married a Miss Laura Francis in 1873. When her brother died in 1883, having no children, the estate was left entirely to his wife. Miss Jenner claimed that her father had, during his life, promised her not only the cottage called Typica and the grounds around it, but also other portions of the estate. Her brother contended that she was only allowed to reside there under sufferance.

Being under the impression that she was deprived of her interest in the Wenvoe Castle estate, Miss Jenner devoted herself to the arduous task of trying to prove her claim.

Not withstanding her poverty, she helped many charitable institutions of Cardiff especially the Infirmary. For some time on 'Infirmary Saturday', she stood at the entrance of Cardiff market and received pence from passers by. The picture shows her with her collecting tin.

She was also one of an active group of suffragettes in Cardiff and was a lifelong philanthropist. The eccentric Miss Jenner was especially proud of her efforts in support of young women facing capital punishment for infanticide. Her boast was that she had saved some fortunate women from the gallows. She passed away on 17 April 1904, only six months before this postcard was sent. (1028)

The Grange, Wenvoe. The Grange was built in 1894 and was occupied by William Nell, a well known Cardiff brewer. In 1920 it was secured by the administrators of the United Services Fund as a temporary home for children of ex-servicemen, and afterwards as a convalescent home for war disabled soldiers. In 1928 it was acquired by the British Legion and converted into a training centre for convalescent ex-servicemen who had been suffering from ailments contracted overseas. (3581)

The Village (No. 1), Wenvoe. The writer of this card describes Wenvoe as a very pretty village. It was certainly very quiet when this picture was taken, c. 1911. (3578)

The Village (No. 2), Wenvoe. This card was sent as a New Year card in 1911 demonstrating the versatility of postcards at that time. The cyclist leaning on his bike is the only observer of our photographer in Wenvoe Village. (3582)

The Old Mill, Dinas Powis. The mill itself was constructed in 1426. It was in use for five centuries. Milling ceased before the Second World War and the millpond was emptied. The mill was converted into a modern house. Above the mill can be seen the castle on the hill with the mock castle below it. The mill was also a farm, with a dutch barn on the left. (2189)

Three

Transport

The Docks, Burry Port. Burry Port is a seaport adjoining the village of Pembray in the old county of Carmarthen. The harbour on the north side of the Burry river was well sheltered. The outer or tidal harbour was fifteen acres in extent. The East Dock was a floating dock with an area of about half an acre, capable of admitting vessels of 1,800 tons. Principal exports were anthracite, coal, fireclay and tinplate. (2841)

Southend, Mumbles. (2939)

The Swansea and Mumbles railway ran from the town of Swansea to the neighbouring Mumbles. It was built in 1804 as an industrial tram road on which horses pulled wagon loads of limestone and coal. The first regular rail passenger service in the world began on this line in 1807. With the passing years Mumbles lost its industrial character and became purely a resort and residential area. As freight all but disappeared, the only traffic available was passengers. The line was electrified in 1929 and had a fleet of tram cars. It closed in 1960.

The Mumbles train. (4805)

The Docks (No. 1), Port Talbot. (3779) What wonderful tall masted ships are in these pictures, c. 1913!

Port Talbot was constituted a separate port on 1 January 1904, having been formally included with Swansea. Exports from the dock were principally coal, manufactured copper, manufactured iron, angle iron, steel plate, coke and patent fuel. Imports were copper, iron ores, pig iron, pitwood and block tin. Note that the bottom picture is the centrepiece of the multiview card of Port Talbot No. 3809.

The Docks (No. 2), Port Talbot. (3780)

General View (No. 3), Barry Dock. (4284)

Barry Dock was formally opened on 18 July 1889. It was mainly used for the exportation of coal. The coal trucks from Tredegar are clearly visible.

General View (No. 5), Barry Dock. (4281)

Penarth Dock, *c.* 1909. This dock was opened in 1865, with an extension in 1884. This was done to relieve the pressure on Cardiff Dock. (2530)

The Pier, Penarth, *c.* 1908. A Campbell's pleasure steamer can be seen stopping at the pier for the residents of Penarth, perhaps on its way to Weston and Ilfracombe. (2530)

Pleasure steamers, off Pier Head, Cardiff. (2971)

The origin of the Campbell's pleasure steamers lies in the nineteenth century, when the family began its steamer services on the River Clyde. In the 1880s the brothers, Peter and Alexander, transferred their business from Glasgow to Bristol. As the popularity of marine excursions flourished in the 1890s, they increased their fleet and started a network of Bristol Channel services. With the outbreak of the First World War, the admiralty requisitioned the thirteen vessels then owned by the company, to be used as mine sweepers. At the end of hostilities the company resumed its services which continued until the declaration of the Second World War, when the Admiralty again requisitioned its the entire fleet of only eleven vessels. After the Second World War a reduced fleet of six vessels survived until 1968.

Pier Head, Cardiff. (2970)

The Railway Station, Hirwain. The station sign reads Hirwain: Junction for Merthyr, on this unnumbered card, *c.* 1918. Hirwain station was on the Vale of Neath railway. (No Number)

Tonypandy from TVR Station, *c.* 1911. This was the junction for the goods only line of the TVR to Clydach Vale. (3528)

The Railway Station, Penrhiwceiber, *c.* 1912. This is a view of the station looking towards Abercynon. It was on the main line of the TVR from Cardiff to Aberdare. It was opened on 1 June 1883, and renamed, Low Level, on 1 July 1924. The last train left on Saturday 14 March 1964 and the station was formally closed on Monday 16 March 1967. (3816)

TVR Railway Station, Nelson, Glam., *c.* 1911. On 1 June 1900 TVR began a passenger service from Pontypridd via the Pont Shon/Norton connection, to its own station at Nelson. Its working life was shortlived, though, and it was closed to passengers on 12 September 1932. (3766)

General View, Rhymney. Coal trucks and numerous advertising signs decorate this magnificent picture of Rhymney station, *c.* 1914. (3906)

The Railway Station. Cwm, *c.* 1911. Travelling up the valley, through Cwm, on the GWR. The next stop was Victoria and then on to Ebbw Vale. (3630)

The Railway Station, Fochriw. A tranquil valley station on the Brecon/Merthyr railway,
c. 1910. (3344)

Rhymney Railway Station, Brithdir. On the Rhymney line, next stop up the valley was Tirphil. Note the railwayman posing on the left. (2773)

The Railway Station, Rogerstone. At Rogerstone, on the Western Valleys line, there was a large marshalling yard which closed towards the end of 1968. The GWR advertise holiday excursions on the station billboards. (4424)

Cross Keys, from the Railway Station. Another station on the Western Valleys line to Ebbw Vale, *c.* 1921. (4380)

The Railway Station and High Street, Argoed, *c.* 1920. George James Taylor was the stationmaster at this stop on the London and North Western line from Blackwood to Ebbw Vale. (4399)

The Railway Station and works, Panteg and Griffithstown, *c.* 1921. This shows the Eastern Valley line of the GWR, from Newport to Pontypool, with the steelworks in the background. (4477)

The Railway Station, Pontnewydd. On the GWR line from Newport, via Caerleon, to Pontypool, *c.* 1911. (3583)

Four
Cardiff

Cardiff, Past and Present. This is one of the six cards in the series, 'Past and Present Cardiff'. The picture in the top left is the Queens Hotel, Pineapple Inn and Rock and Fountain Inn on St Mary Street in 1883. The bottom right is the same view with the caption 'Present Day' – The present day was of course, around 1906.

Cardiff, Past and Present, *c.* 1906. This is another card in the series, showing The Spital Cottages in 1883. These were in Crockherbertown which by 1906 was Queen Street. The Spital (or Spitle), which used to stand nearby, was a medieval leper hospital, which later became private property.

Twyn, St Fagans. These two beautiful thatched cottages stood in St Fagans, *c.* 1909. (3105)

Fairwater, near Cardiff. Fairwater was a rural community when this was taken around 1912. Note the fields on the hill in the background. (3740)

Llandaff fields showing the Cathedral and Bishop's Palace, *c.* 1910. The Cathedral and Bishop's Palace are in the background and there is a drinking fountain by the large tree on the right. (3041)

Cardiff Road, Llandaff. There are two vehicles almost forming a road block in Llandaff, *c.* 1911. Note the public telephone outside Edwards the cash chemists. The telephone number was 146. (3743)

Conway Road, Cardiff, *c.* 1909. This picture shows a lamp post in the middle of the road as well as several unsupervised children. How times have changed! (3060)

St Mary's church, King Road, Cardiff. A parked handcart and a horse and cart are the only traffic in Kings Road, *c.* 1910. (3054)

Romilly Road, Cardiff. The lady who posted this card was having a nice holiday in Romilly crescent in 1910. From the look of the picture it was certainly a quiet holiday. (3059)

Fitzhamon Embankment, Riverside, Cardiff. The young lady is wearing a hat and scarf to protect her against the cold in this picture of the embankment, c. 1910. Canton Bridge is in the background. (3028)

Clare Gardens, Riverside, Cardiff. What peace and tranquillity in Clare Gardens, c. 1910. (3031)

Cowbridge Road (No. 2), Cardiff. A few cyclists are the only traffic on Cowbridge Road, *c.* 1909. Note the dress of the lady on the corner, to the left. (2906)

Bute Street (No. 2), Cardiff. A gentleman carefully makes his way down the stairs on the tram under the watchful gaze of the conductor, *c.* 1911. This area was in the heart of the dockland, and the picture shows a veritable hive of activity. (3239)

The Hayes, Cardiff, *c.* 1912. At 10.49, a No. 56 tram heads for the Pier Head, past Morgan & Co. through the Hayes. There are in fact four trams in the picture. They even went in pairs then! (3135)

Church Street, Cardiff, c. 1910. Church Street was not a traffic free precinct then, but only one car is travelling toward the High Street. How did Mr Bush get this angle? Was he on the top of a tram perhaps? The tower of St John's church is in the background. (3100)

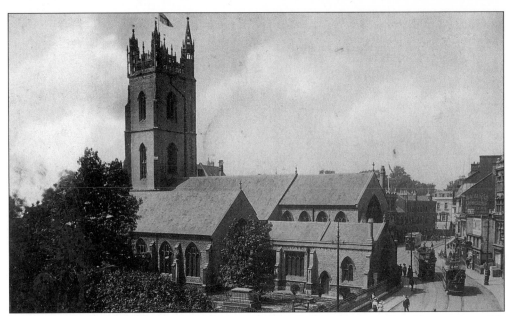

St John's church, Cardiff. It is interesting to note that this was sent as a New Year card to a Mr Smart at Chalford, near Stroud. It is noteworthy that in this picture there are still buildings in front of the castle. These were not demolished until 1923. (3098)

Queens Street, Cardiff. A postman on a bike, two other cyclists, an open backed van, a tram, a hand cart and two horse drawn vehicles form the entire traffic content of Queens Street, c. 1923. Quite different to today! (4866)

Park Hall Buildings, Queen Street, Cardiff. Lassams advertise a great sale on the corner of Park Place, *c.* 1911. (3695)

King Edward Avenue, Cathays Park, Cardiff, *c.* 1913. The man on the steps to the far right seems to have more than a passing interest in our photographer. (3976)

The Bowling Green, Grange Gardens (No. 2), Cardiff, *c.* 1911. The Bowling Green was opened on 23 June 1906, at a cost of £20. Present was 'a large gathering of aldermen and councillors and many ladies in attendance'. (3505)

Channel and Holmsview, Rhymney, near Cardiff. Dorothy lived in the house marked with a cross on this picture of Rhymney, *c.* 1913. The height of the pavement above the road is unbelievable. (3823)

(Bathing) Roath Park Lake, Cardiff. The oarsman manages a pose in the boat flanked by bathers at Roath Park lake, *c.* 1910. (3126)

Cardiff Road, Llanishen. A solitary vehicle wends its way down Cardiff Road, *c.* 1912. (3316)

The Village, Llanishen. This is one of the early 'Bush Series' colour photographs, showing a very smart policeman, complete with walking stick, keeping an eye on our photographer. It is one of very few Bush Series in colour. (7502 R)

The Free Library and Park Road, Whitchurch, c. 1910. The library was built with financial assistance from Andrew Carnegie. (3024)

Rhubina Hill, Whitchurch. (3876). Rhubina and Thornhill were strictly rural when these pictures were taken in around 1913.

Thornhill From Wenallt Road, Whitchurch. (3872)

Cardiff Road (No. 1), Radyr. Here is a peaceful village scene in Radyr, *c.* 1909. (2924)

Five

The Valleys:
Rhondda, Cynon, Taff, Rhymney and Ebbw

Meet of the hounds at Castle Coch, attended by Lord Ninian Stuart. The huntsmen, hounds and foot followers assembled here at Castle Coch in around 1909. (2967)

The Canal Lock House, Taffs Well, *c.* 1926. The Merthyr to Cardiff canal was opened on 10 February 1794 for the purpose of bringing finished iron from Merthyr to Cardiff Docks. (6048)

Glanllyn, Taffs Well, *c.* 1909. An unbelievable view now of Glanllyn, Taffs Well. (3076)

Glyngwyn Street (No. 2), Miskin. A long skirted lady watches Mr Bush take this bleak picture of Miskin, *c.* 1913. (3820)

Bridge Street, Pontypridd, *c.* 1911. Of note are the two bridges which cross the River Taff in the background of this picture. (3546)

Oxford Street, Mountain Ash, *c.* 1911. William Hughes was the proprietor of The New Inn opposite William Jones the chemist at 9, Oxford Street, when this picture of Mountain Ash was taken. Note the dray horses pulling the cart delivering to the New Inn. (3644)

Penrhiwceiber Road (No. 3), Penrhiwceiber, *c.* 1911. (3654)

These are two pictures of Penrhiwceiber Road, Penrhiwceiber, both with the same caption and both taken from almost the same place but on different dates. Above, the names of the shops can clearly be seen as well as the name on the horse drawn cart: R. J. Heath, pianofortes and organs. Below, the tradesmen in their aprons pose outside their various establishments.

Penrhiwceiber Road (No. 3), Penrhiwceiber, *c.* 1912. (3819)

The Park, Penycraig, (sic), should read The Park, Penygraig. Note how Bush has caught the little girl trying to reach the water fountain in about 1911. (3524)

High Street, Treorchy. A lad climbs on a horse and cart in High Street, *c.* 1911. (3512)

The Revd D. Rhagfyr Jones is seen in the insert, above the Welsh congregational church, Bethania chapel, *c.* 1908. Note that there is another straw boater! (2669)

Glyncolly Road, Treorchy. A sweeping brush lies abandoned, perhaps by the two posing ladies, in Glyncolly Road, *c.* 1911. The Revd D. R. Jones in photograph 2669 also lives in this road. (3514)

Ely Street, Tonypandy. A horse drawn cart from The White Star cleaners completely blocks the road in Ely Street, *c.* 1911. (3602)

The Square, Sherwood, Llwynpia. It is interesting to note that in around 1911 there was no ban on tobacco advertising in the square at Llwynyia! (3537)

St Peter's church, Pentre. The Revd Canon William Lewis was vicar and Revd Daniel George Warner was curate at St Peter's church, c. 1911. (3543)

The Square, Nelson, Glam. The policeman who is standing proudly outside the police station could be Walter Kelland, who was the sergeant there in 1912. (3767)

Penygraig Road, Penygraig. A valley road in Penygraig, c. 1914. (3953)

Duffryn Terrace, Elliots Town. A young lad clutches a wicker basket in the centre of Duffryn Terrace, *c.* 1914. (3936)

Trehafod Road (No. 2), Trehafod. A cart advertising 'fresh fish daily' wends its way up Trehafod Road, *c.* 1913. (3834)

The Square, Clydach, *c.* 1911. In the square, a horse trough, an advertisement for The Globe showing *Anthony and Cleopatra*, the Jones Bros Emporium, and The Cooks Arms, all grace the scene. (3665)

3629. Station Terrace, Cwm.   Ernest T. Bush.

Station Terrace, Cwm. A view of Station Terrace, Cwm, *c.* 1911. (3629)

Queens Crescent, Rhymney. Probably another straw boatered member of the Bush entourage poses with two lads in Queens Crescent, *c.* 1913. (3907)

High Street (No. 1), Blackwood. M. Love house furnisher's, situated next to Blackwood post office, ply their trade in High Street, *c.* 1913. Note the rows of shoes hanging outside Briggs emporium. (3865)

Park Road, Hengoed, *c.* 1910. (3617)

The new parish church, Llanhilleth, Aberbeeg, *c.* 1914. The new church was erected in 1910, at a cost of over £6,000. It was built from stone, in the style of the late fourteenth century. It consisted of a chancel, nave, north and south transepts, the organ chamber and vestries and it had seating for 500. (3627)

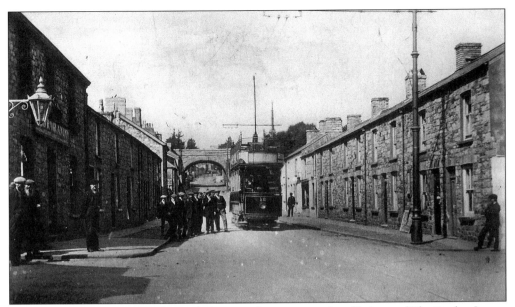

The Stocks, High Street, Cefn Coed. It seems that everyone has filed out of The Raglan Inn to pose for their photograph in the High Street Cefn Coed, *c.* 1919. (4022)

Thomas Street, Abertridwr. A lady, looking like she has just stepped off a 1990s style magazine, stands on the corner in Thomas Street next to a lady carrying a baby in a shawl. The shop window of J. Samson, baker and confectioner, advertises 'The Last Days of Pompeii'. The National Provincial Bank can just be seen on the right. (3716)

High Street, Llanbradach. You could just imagine this cyclist going 'weeeeee' as he travels downhill past Frank Leggit, the jeweller at 3 High Street, *c*. 1913. (3929)

Piccadilly Square, Caerphilly. The Piccadilly Inn on the left is mentioned in an 1829 document 'Cardiff Guide and Directory', and probably gave its name to the square. Again we have a smartly dressed man in a straw boater looking most out of place striding up the middle of Piccadilly Square, *c*. 1912. (3838)

Six

Monmouthshire

Church Street, Ebbw Vale. Masters & Co. clothiers at No. 20, The Home and Colonial at No. 22, Mrs Elizabeth Jorden bookmakers, at No. 26, English and Colonial Meat Company at No. 49 and John Headingly family butcher at No. 51, were just a few of the businesses in Church Street in about 1921. (4350)

Bethcar Street, Ebbw Vale. The Bon Marche occupies a prominent site in Bethcar Street, *c.* 1921. (4351)

High Street, Cross Keys. A quiet High Street, *c.* 1921. (4379)

Gladstone Street, Cross Keys, *c.* 1921. A solitary horse and cart makes its way down Gladstone Street, past the hoarding advertising seats at The Coliseum for 6d ($2\frac{1}{2}$p) and 1/3 ($6\frac{1}{2}$p). (4375)

Chatham, Machen. Machen was composed of twin villages, Upper and Lower Machen. For a hundred years Lower Machen was a small lead mining settlement under the control of Caerleon. Here slaves lived in barracks under military command. (4431)

Tredegar Street (No. 1), Risca. (4381) Two pictures of Tredegar Street, Risca, c. 1921, inventively numbered 1 and 2. Note the hatters in the distance in No. 1 and the central cinema, with proprietor David Richards in No. 2.

Tredegar Street (No. 2), Risca. (4382)

St John's church, Rogerstone. The church of St John was erected in 1888, at a cost of £2,370. (4423)

Tregwillyn Road, Rogerstone. Jane Crabb was the beer retailer at The Royal Oak Inn, in Tregwillyn Road when this picture was taken, *c.* 1920. (4419)

Newport, Mon. One of the first multiview cards ever produced by Mr Bush. The five pictures on this card have all also been produced as individual cards. The top left is a card reproduced in this volume, see No. 2894, p. 95.

BRIDGE AND CASTLE

BRIDGE

BELLE VUE PARK

The Locks, Alteryn, Newport, Mon. These were situated on a branch of the Monmouthshire canal from Crumlin to Malpas. The canal was opened to transport finished iron from the valleys to the port at Newport. The Crumlin branch was closed in 1947, but has found a new lease of life in recent years as a tourist attraction. (3251)

Commercial Street, Newport. The clock on the old Town Hall and the Westgate Hotel are clearly visible on this view of Commercial Street from Westgate Square, c. 1909. Note the different styles in hats. (2481)

High Street (No. 2), Newport, Mon. I wonder if there is a collective noun for banks. A deposit of banks perhaps? Here we have The United Counties Bank Ltd, The Midland Bank Ltd and The National Provincial Bank Ltd, all at the same road junction in Newport High Street, *c.* 1912. The tram displays an advertisement for the Empire in Charles Street. (2894)

Bridge Street, Newport, Mon. Bridge Street before the Pizza Hut, *c.* 1912. In the centre is The Queens Hotel, where Mrs Edith Morgan was proprietor, and The Lyceum Theatre on the right where Mr Sidney Cooper was Lessee and manager. (3769)

Clarence Place, Newport. Cadbury's chocolate, Rountree's chocolate and Rountree's pastilles are all advertised outside the establishment of Harold Paxton, the tobacconist of Clarence Place, *c.* 1908. It is noteworthy that neither The Odeon, The Coliseum nor The Cenotaph have yet been built. (2488)

Caerleon Road, Newport, Mon. A tram heading for Newport docks passes James & Harris monumental masons, on the corner of Turner Street, *c.* 1910. (3772)

High Street (No. 2), Abersychan. Umbrellas were repaired, drapery was available from Daniel Davies, confectionery and hairdressing from Mr Wyndham Harris and alcoholic beverages from Mr Herbert Brown, proprietor at The Bell Hotel in the High Street Abersychan, *c.* 1910. (3134)

Broad Street, Abersychan. The Union Hotel, complete with carriages and occupants, immediately catches the eye in this picture of Broad Street, Abersychan, *c.* 1910. (3156)

Station Road, Pontnewydd. Poulton & Whiting builders and contractors, James Samuel grocer, Bertram Theodore Jarratt insurance agent and The Kings Head public house, all conducted their businesses in Station Road, *c.* 1911. (3560)

The Five Locks Bridge, Pontnewydd. Mr Bush even manages to find three posers on the bridge over the Brecon and Monmouthshire canal, 1911. (3586)

Pontrhydyrun chapel, near Pontnewydd. Pontrhydyrun was a hamlet, one mile north of Pontnewydd. This picture shows the chapel in about 1911. (3590)

Commercial Street, Pontnewydd. A local delivery boy from Edward James Richards the grocer, carries a customised basket in Commercial Street, while a railwayman looks intently on, c. 1902. This card is from the early Bush Series. (1013)

Pontypool and District hospital, Pontnewynydd. Built in 1903, at a cost of £8,000, Pontypool and District hospital was constructed on a site presented by John Capel Hanbury Esq. It was described at its opening as being 'an edifice of stone with 24 beds'. (2872)

Windsor Road, Griffithstown. A fine picture of Griffithstown, in about 1921, with the grocer's shop of Herbert James Thomas, at Nos. 59 and 60 Windsor Road, clearly visible on the right of the picture. (4475)

Crane Street, Pontypool. Mr John Davies was manager at the Ship hotel on the left of Crane Street, *c.* 1921. Note the Manchester House showrooms on the right. (4345)

Commercial Street, Pontypool, *c.* 1921. A busy street scene in Pontypool where refreshments and iced drinks could be obtained at Mrs Sarah Osbourne's refreshment rooms on the right of the picture. Other traders included Eastmans family butcher's and Fowlers draper's shop. (4344)

THE CASTLE.

GENERAL VIEW and SUGAR LOAF

Enjoying ourselves at Abergavenny, published around 1924. A multiview of Abergavenny. Although no cards with a single picture of Abergavenny have yet been seen, the picture (top right) of Abergavenny Castle has appeared in a guide book of the area. It seems that the

THE CASTLE (*ENTRANCE*)

ENJOYING
OURSELVES·AT

ABERGAVENNY

5782   ·ERNEST·T·BUSH·

photographs included in this multiview help to account for the missing pictures in the listing.
(5782)

The bridge, Usk. The name 'Usk' is derived from the Gaelic 'Visge', which means 'water'. This is an excellent view of the stone bridge with its four arches as it spans the River Usk. (3356)

Monnow Bridge, Monmouth. Another stone bridge, but with three arches spanning the River Monnow. The ancient gateway on the bridge has two storeys with a projecting garde robe and a sloping roof. (3366)

Rolls Memorial, Monmouth. In the background of this picture is the Shire Hall in Agincourt Square which is an edifice of stone in the Ionic style, with an open arcaded basement and an upper storey. In the arched recess is a full sized statue in armour of King Henry V, who was born in Monmouth Castle in August 1387. The memorial itself is to the Hon. Charles Stewart Rolls, M.A., F.R.G.S., F.R.Met.S., A.M.Inst.M.E.; who was Captain of the London section army motor reserve; technical managing director of Rolls Royce Ltd, British motor manufacturers and third son of the first Baron Llangattock. He was born in London on 27 August 1877, and was educated at Eton and Trinity College, Cambridge. He graduated in engineering with a B.A. in 1898 and a M.A. in 1902. He was a pioneer in the introduction of automobilism into England in 1896, and drove a motor car before the abolition of the 'red flag' regulation. He was also a certified aeronaut, owing a balloon aeroplane and making over 160 balloon ascents. His local residence was The Hendre, Monmouth, and he died on 12 July 1910. (3368)

Tintern Abbey (No. 4). This is one of a series of photographs taken by Mr Bush of the famous Abbey at Tintern which was founded by Walter Fitz-Richard de Clare, Lord of Chepstow, in 1131 and was dedicated to St Mary. It was founded for the Cistercian order. In the sixteenth century, Catholicism was outlawed and the country's abbeys and monasteries were dissolved. At its dissolution Tintern Abbey had only thirteen inmates. (3326)

Undy Road, Magor, c. 1921. A young lad sits on a motor cycle outside the Wheatsheaf in Magor, where the proprietor was Abel Wood Williams. The inn is still flourishing today, although the surroundings have dramatically changed. (4577)

Seven
Industry

Plymouth colliery, Troedyrhiw, *c*. 1908. This was a nineteenth-century mine where an eleven-year-old boy was killed in 1870. It was worked in the last century to feed the Plymouth iron works. (2721)

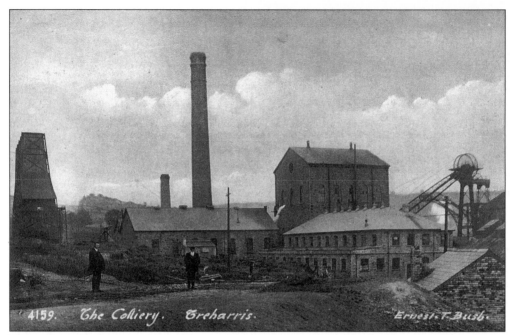

The colliery, Treharris, *c.* 1920. There is not much activity, and in the foreground is a clue to why, with two men dressed up in their Sunday best.

Cwmaman Fforchwen colliery. This colliery, together with Cwmaman colliery and Trewen, was worked by the Cwmaman Coal Company in the early decades of this century. Sinking commenced in 1850 but was abandoned after 60 yards. The pit was finally completed in 1897 at a depth of 360 yards, with mining started in 1900. It employed 1,160 men in 1913 and was later absorbed into Cwmaman colliery. (4133)

Nantewlaeth colliery, near Cymmer. Gibbs Navigation Colliery Ltd opened this pit near Cymmer in West Glamorgan at the beginning of the century. It was worked until 1948 and was then closed by the National Coal Board. (4218)

Risca pits, Cross Keys. The Risca pits were sunk in 1878 to a depth of 1,009 feet by the London & South Wales Colliery Company. It was later owned, first by United National Collieries, then by Ocean & United National and finally by the National Coal Board who closed the colliery in July 1966. In 1913, Risca pits employed 1,117 men. On 15 July 1880, an explosion killed 119 men and boys. One journalistic statement of the time, perhaps reflecting the underlying social climate, reported the severe financial loss incurred by the mine owner. With the death of 28 pit ponies, the value was estimated at about £1,000. (4377)

Celynen colliery (north), Newbridge, *c.* 1920. This colliery which produced over 40 million tons of coal in its lifetime, mainly from Black Vein Seam, was sunk by the Newport and Abercarn Black Vein Steam Coal Company, and started work in 1914. It was closed in 1985. (4388)

Navigation colliery (No. 2), Bedwas, *c.* 1920. The Navigation Steam Coal Company commenced sinking in 1909 and the first coal was produced in 1912. By 1913 it employed 500 men. It was taken over by The Bedwas Navigation Colliery Company in 1921 and by The National Coal Board in 1947. It was closed in 1985. (4433)

Nut and bolt works, Cwmbran, *c.* 1921. This was part of Guest, Keen & Nettlefolds Ltd. (4449)

Baldwin's works, Panteg, *c.* 1921. Baldwin's works, which was later to become Richard Thomas & Baldwin's, manufactured steel and galvanized iron. (4471)

Tredomen engineering works, Ystrad Mynach. Four men arrive for work at Ystrad Mynach, *c.* 1922.

Ocean colliery, Blaengarw. Three workmen have climbed the tower, centre right, to watch our photographer at work. (3855)

Cwmcynon colliery, Penrhiwceiber. Situated near Mountain Ash, this was the most southerly of Nixons Navigation Coal Company's collieries. Opened in 1895, it produced steam coal until it was closed by The National Coal Board in 1949. In 1913, it employed 1,882 men. (3817)

Penrhiwceiber colliery, Penrhiwceiber, c. 1914. This pit was sunk in 1872 and was worked by The Penrikyber Navigation Coal Company prior to nationalization in 1947. In 1913 it employed 1i944 men. It was closed by The National Coal Board in 1986. (3811)

Oakdale colliery, Blackwood. This pit, the last deep mine to work in the county of Gwent, was sunk in 1908 by the Oakdale Navigation Company to a depth of 2,238 feet. It was closed in 1990.

Glenavon colliery, Blaengarw, c. 1914. It was a level opened by The Glynogwr Collieries Ltd and was worked from 1909 to 1949. In 1914 it employed 173 men underground. (3850)

Abergorky colliery, Treorchy. (3517) Abergorky colliery, above, was one of Burn, Yeat & Brown's first ventures into mining. The colliery was later worked by the Ocean Coal Company. Some of the miners can be seen at the pithead below. By 1920 it was employing 1,800 men.

The Pithead, Abergorky colliery, Treorchy. (3518)

Coedely pit, Thomastown, *c.* 1911. While mining provided employment for local inhabitants, this scene, with the hills in the background, shows the effect mining had on the countryside. (3505)

Glamorgan colliery, Llwynpia. Also known as the Scotch colliery, it was opened from 1861 by The Glamorgan Coal Company. By 1910 it was part of the Cambrian Combine with the No. 1 pit employing 1,712 men, the No. 2 pit, 1,539 men and the No. 6 pit 656 men. They were all closed in the 1930s. (3532)

Gelli colliery, Gelli. Gelli colliery was opened around 1878 by Thomas & Griffiths, but was mainly worked by the Cory Brothers Ltd. In 1913 it employed 296 men. The colliery encompassed both household and steam coal pits. It was closed by the National Coal Board in January 1962. (3542)

Cambrian colliery, Clydach Vale. The Cambrian colliery was a series of four pits opened from 1873 by the Cambrian Collieries Ltd. They were later owned by the Powell Dyffryn Combine before being nationalized in 1947. The last pit was closed in 1966. Two serious explosions occurred at this colliery, one on 10 March 1905 and the other on 17 May 1963. The accidents killed 31 miners each. (3557)

The Marine colliery, Cwm, *c.* 1910. The Marine colliery was opened in 1889 by The Ebbw Vale Steel, Iron and Coal Company. In 1913 it employed a massive 2,407 men but disaster struck on 1 March 1927 when an explosion killed 52 men. The colliery was taken over with the rest of the Ebbw Vales Company's mines by Partridge Jones and John Paron & Company in 1935, and then by The National Coal Board in 1947. It was closed by British Coal in March 1989. (3632)

Nixons Navigation colliery, Mountain Ash, *c.* 1914. This colliery was sunk between 1853 and 1860. In 1913 it employed 1,095 men and was worked until the 1920s by The Nixon Navigation Coal Company. After the 1920s, it continued its life as a maintenance depot. (3682)

The Pit, Aberaman, *c.* 1910. This was one of the earliest pits to open in the area. It was opened in 1847 by Crawshay Bailey, and was bought, in 1866, by Sir George Elliot to form part of the new Powell Dyffryn Steam Coal Company. By 1913 it was employing 1,095 men. It was closed in November 1962 by The National Coal Board. (3017)

Fernhill colliery, Treherbert *c.* 1912. Opened by the Fernhill Colliery Company in 1871, it was employing 1,127 men by 1920. It was closed by The National Coal Board in 1966. (3049)

McClaren colliery (No. 1), Abertysswg, *c.* 1911. Sinking was commenced in August 1897 by the Tredegar Iron Company and the colliery was named after Sir Charles Mclaren. On 3 September 1902 an explosion killed 16 men and injured 21 others. In 1913 the McClaren colliery employed 1,833 men. (3004)

Coegnant colliery, Caerau, *c.* 1908. Sunk in 1882, by the Llynfi Coal and Iron Company, this colliery employed 1,900 men by 1913. It was closed by the National Coal Board in 1982. (2347)

Eight

Outside South Wales

Broad Street from the bridge, Newtown. A superb picture of the approach to Newtown via the bridge over the river, *c*. 1925. (5662)

THE CHECKERS INN

BROAD STREET

Having a high time at Newtown. Another card in Mr Bush's series of multiviews. None of the pictures comprising this multiview have yet been recorded as a separate postcard. (5778)

THE INFIRMARY

HAVING·A·HIGH·
TIME·AT

NEWTOWN

5778   ·ERNEST·T·BUSH·

Park Crescent, Llandrindod Wells. Ernest Bush is really far from home now, *c.* 1925. Note James Barkley fruiterer, in the centre of the picture and the post office on the right. Don't you just love the cyclist in his plus fours! (5676)

The Park and Pump Rooms, Llandrindod Wells, *c.* 1925. The pump rooms had completely fitted bathrooms attached. The waters and baths were considered to be 'particularly efficacious in cases of liver complaint, dyspepsia, gout, rheumatic gout, rheumatism, calculus, kidney diseases and general debility'. (2463)

Alpine Bridge, Llandrindod Wells. A young lady looks wistfully over the Alpine Bridge at Llandrindod Wells, *c.* 1909. (2469)

The Mid Wales mental hospital, Talgarth, *c.* 1920. This was the mental hospital for the counties of Breconshire and Radnorshire, built at a cost of £140,000 and opened on 18 February 1903. (4501)

The Square, Talgarth. The delivery vehicle of Evans Stores, who traded in the square, is clearly seen on the left of the picture, *c.* 1924. Also note the wonderful garage vehicle, complete with Shell advertising, on the right. (4499)

Nine

Additions and Amendments

Following the publication of Volume 1, a number of cards previously unknown to me have been kindly brought to my attention. These, together with a few amendments, are listed here. A full listing appears in Volume 1. The two lists, together, provide a record of all the cards published that have been brought to my attention. It is not claimed that it is complete, however, and I am always very pleased to be notified of cards that are in other collections but not listed here.

1028	Miss Gertrude Jenner (Copyright), Wenvoe
1028	The Old Thatched Cottage, Dinas Powis
2174	Roath Park, Cardiff
2175	Cardiff Road, Llanishen
2183	Cwrt yr Ala, Dinas Powis
2197	The church, Wenvoe
2311	General View, Aberfan
2384	Station Road (No. 2), Llanishen
2462	Penpych mountain
2476	Church Road, Whitchurch
2512	The parish church, Llantwit Fardre
2551	St Dingats church, New Tredegar
2552	General View, New Tredegar
2560	High Street (No.3), Cefn
2664	The colliery, Llanbradach
2686	The Cross & Vicarage, Wenvoe
2709	Hawthorn, Rhydfelin
2772	West Elliot colliery, Brithdir
2975	Fitzhamon embankment, Cardiff
3154	High Street (No.2), Abersychan
3160	Victoria Schools and General View, Abersychan
3162	General View from the woods, Abersychan
3226	Golf links, Pontnewydd
3276	General View, Aberfan
3503	Tynycoed Terrace, Thomastown
3509	Marshfield (No.1)
3564	Commercial Street (No.2), Pontnewydd
3573	General View (No. 2), Rhydfelan

3586	The Five Locks bridge, Pontnewydd
3595	Rhydfelan (Showing Ebanezar chapel)
3596	Glantaff, from Rhydfelan
3696	Francis Street, Abertridwr
3697	Eglwysilan church, Abertridwr
3705	Maesywern Road, Pencoed
3741	Ely, near Cardiff
3807	The Craig, Llanhilleth
3837	Pontygwyndy Road, Caerphilly
3846	St Martin's church, Caerphilly
3993	The Welsh Metropolitan War Hospital, Whitchurch
4052	The Infants school, Abergwynfi
4053	St Gabriel's church, Abergwynfi
4055	Glyncorrog colliery
4097	Broad Street (No. 1), Blaenavon
4125	The parish church, Llandebie
4152	Fox Street (No. 1), Treharris
4154	The Park and bandstand, Treharris
4288	Pebble beach, Barry
4314	Clydach Valley, Brynmawr
4405	The viaduct, Crumlin
4407	Crumlin and Viaduct
4426	Church and War Memorial, Machen
4443	Ynysyddu
4447	Victoria Street, Cwmbran
4448	The railway station, Cwmbran
4453	Llantarnum Abbey (No.1)
4476	Commercial Street, Griffithstown
4496	The Welsh National Sanatarium (No.1), Talgarth
4724	The Cenotaph, Aberdare
4727	The Public Hall, Aberaman
4728	Belmont Terrace, Aberaman
4781	Caerphilly and District Miners Hospital, Caerphilly
4790	War Memorial, Whitchurch
4801	Bracelet Bay, Mumbles
4802	Limeslade Bay, Mumbles
4887	Singleton University, Swansea
4895	New Road and Mumbles Head
5258	Swiss Valley, Llanelly
5260	Station Road, Llanelly
5477	The Garth, Taffs Well
5789	Greetings & Best Wishes from Cardiff
5793	Greetings from Wenvoe
5830	Foreland Road, Whitchurch
6043	Alexandra Park, Penarth
6046	The Ferry Bridge, Taffs Well
6049	Gwalod-Y-Garth, Taffs Well
6050	Pontshonphillips and Garth Hill, Taffs Well
6050	The Ferry Bridge and Garth Hill, Taffs Well
6070	General View and Ocean colliery, Abergwynfi
5004R	The top of Station Road, Llanishen
5006R	The Village, Llanishen